LATINOS IN THE LIMELIGHT

Christina Aguilera	John Leguizamo
Antonio Banderas	Jennifer Lopez
Jeff Bezos	Ricky Martin
Oscar De La Hoya	Pedro Martinez
Cameron Diaz	Freddie Prinze Jr.
Scott Gomez	Carlos Santana
Salma Hayek	Selena
Enrique Iglesias	Sammy Sosa

CHELSEA HOUSE PUBLISHERS

LATINOS
IN THE
LIMELIGHT

Cameron Díaz

Kieran Scott

CHELSEA HOUSE PUBLISHERS
Philadelphia

Frontis: *Refusing to rely simply on her stunning good looks, Cameron Diaz has built a stellar acting career based on unusual roles and remarkable talent.*

Produced by
21st Century Publishing and Communications, Inc.
New York, New York
http://www.21cpc.com

CHELSEA HOUSE PUBLISHERS

Editor in Chief: Sally Cheney
Production Manager: Pamela Loos
Art Director: Sara Davis
Director of Photography: Judy L. Hasday
Managing Editor: James D. Gallagher
Senior Production Editor: J. Christopher Higgins
Publishing Coordinator: James McAvoy
Project Editor: Anne Hill

The Chelsea House World Wide Web address is
http://www.chelseahouse.com

First Printing

1 3 5 7 9 8 6 4 2

Library of Congress Cataloging-in-Publication Data

Scott, Kieran, 1974–
  Cameron Diaz / Kieran Scott.
    p. cm. – (Latinos in the limelight)
  Includes filmography, bibliographical references, and index.
  ISBN 0-7910-6108-6 (hardcover) — ISBN 0-7910-6109-4 (pbk.)
    1. Diaz, Cameron—Juvenile literature 2. Motion picture actors and actresses—United States—Biography—Juvenile literature. 3. Hispanic American motion picture actors and actresses—United States—Biography—Juvenile literature. [1. Diaz, Cameron. 2. Actors and actresses. 3. Women—Biography.] I. Title. II. Series.

PN2287.D4633 S385 2000
791.43'028'092—dc21
[B]
                                                              00—059630
                                                                  CIP
                                                                  AC

CONTENTS

1

BEING CAMERON DIAZ

At the 72nd annual Academy Awards ceremony in March 2000, Cameron Diaz showed up in a beautiful designer dress, looking slinky and gorgeous, just like she always does when red carpets are involved. Viewers of the award show telecast might have had a hard time believing she was the same person who had acted in the film she was there to support. In *Being John Malkovich*, Cameron, one of her generation's most adored beauties, was transformed into someone unrecognizable—the bizarre, semi-desperate character of Lotte Schwartz.

For the role, Cameron had to completely transform herself. Lotte was emotionally weak as well as physically plain, with brown eyes, frizzy brown hair, pasty skin, and frumpy clothes. At the beginning of the movie, she was quiet and shy and didn't have much confidence. One online reviewer even said, "Casting is flawless with Cameron Diaz made up to be about as unattractive as she possibly could."

Lotte was nothing like Cameron Diaz. And that's exactly why Cameron wanted to play her.

Few people could imagine elegant beauty Cameron Diaz appearing as frumpy and insecure, but that's exactly what she did as Lotte Schwartz in the critically acclaimed movie Being John Malkovich. *"That's the thing about making movies—you get to do something you've never done before," she said.*

"Once I got the part (Director Spike Jonze and I) sort of started putting Lotte together and it is really the first time that I've played someone *completely* different than me. She's physically nothing like me and really as a person not much like me," Cameron said with a laugh.

All her life, Cameron has steered clear of the norm. She's been daring, outspoken, and brash. Playing Lotte was just another one of those courageous moves.

While most budding stars would follow up a surprise hit like 1998's *There's Something about Mary* with another high-profile role, Cameron doesn't choose parts with money and publicity in mind. She just wants to have fun and do interesting projects. That was a huge part of her decision to make *Being John Malkovich*. Another reason was that she and costar Catherine Keener had become friends when Cameron worked on *My Best Friend's Wedding* (1997) with Catherine's husband, Dermott Mulroney.

So when *Being John Malkovich* came along, Cameron explained: "My agent said, 'You have to read this script—it sounds like something you would love. And Catherine is doing it and John Cusack is doing it and John Malkovich is playing himself and there's this director Spike Jonze who everybody thinks is amazing.'"

It was no wonder that Cameron's agent thought she'd like the script. She'd been in some original, even bizarre, movies before. In *A Life Less Ordinary*, Cameron and Ewan McGregor were brought together by a couple of angels who had to make a love connection or be banished from heaven. In *Feeling Minnesota*, Cameron's character ditched her husband seconds after their wedding to run off with the groom's brother,

played by Keanu Reeves. And in her role in *Very Bad Things*, Cameron again got married but had to kill Christian Slater's character just to get to the altar.

Being John Malkovich, however, was probably the most unusual of any of these films. In it, Cameron's character (among others) gets to find out what it's like to be in John Malkovich's body. (The actor, who also starred in *The Man in the Iron Mask* with Leonardo DiCaprio, decided to play himself because he loved the script so much.) In order to get inside Malkovich, though, Lotte had to crawl through a tiny door and get sucked through a slimy, muddy tunnel. Then,

Working with the cast of Being John Malkovich presented Cameron with unusual opportunities, including working with a monkey and spending many hours in a cold, slimy tube.

whenever she left Malkovich's body, she would find herself dumped out on the grass next to the New Jersey Turnpike.

Lotte gets obsessed with being John Malkovich and wants to do it over and over again. At one point in the movie, her husband, played by John Cusack, wants to keep her from entering the tunnel, so he locks her up in a cage with a monkey!

It sounds completely strange—and it is. Cameron spent much of the movie shoot covered with mud and stooped over. But as long as a project sounds fun to Cameron, she wants the role. During the making of the movie, and for months after when she was promoting it, Cameron would laugh when she told stories about the odd sets and the cold, slimy tube she had to slide around in.

Little did Cameron know that playing Lotte would be more than just another entertaining shoot. She would actually learn a lot from looking so different on a daily basis. When she was dressed up as Lotte on the set, people she had been talking to moments earlier as Cameron wouldn't recognize her. Cameron found people treated her in a whole new way . . . and it wasn't necessarily a bad thing.

"There were guys on the set who, as a blonde, would never look at me. And as Lotte, they were more curious about me," Cameron reported. "Everybody has a different taste and a different desire for certain types of people. . . . I was having different types of people engage me, which was a really great and enriching experience for me."

So rather than taking the road most traveled and snagging a part in a romantic comedy or a surefire blockbuster, Cameron took a

smaller role in a less-known movie with a tight budget—and had a fun as well as educational experience in the process. That would have been enough to satisfy this self-defined adventure-seeker. But then the praise started rolling in.

Cameron was nominated for many awards for her role in *Being John Malkovich.* She and costar Catherine Keener were both nominated for Best Supporting Actress at the Golden Globe Awards. Cameron was also nominated for a Golden Satellite Award (handed out by the International Press Association), an American Comedy Award, and a Screen Actors' Guild Award. Cameron didn't take home any statuettes for playing Lotte, but even through her losses, her grace and good nature came through. All she could talk about was how

Cameron jokes with director Spike Jonze at the 2000 MTV Movie Awards, where Jones won Best New Filmmaker for Being John Malkovich. *From left: actress Catherine Keener; Spike Jonze, holding his award; Cameron's older sister, Chimene; and Cameron Diaz.*

grateful she was to have had the opportunity to make such an interesting and innovative film.

"That's the thing about making movies—you get to do something you've never done before," Cameron said. "I've never been pulled through John Malkovich's subconscious tube which happens to be slimy and muddy. And I've never spent two weeks on a set that was four-foot-seven . . . so for me, and I think for everyone, it was a lot of fun."

The other people involved in the film were also honored. *Being John Malkovich* was nominated for a Golden Globe Award as Best Film in a Comedy or Musical, and its director, Spike Jonze, was nominated for an Academy Award as Best Director. The film won the grand prize at the 25th Deuville (France) Festival of American Cinema, the Best Picture Award from the National Society of Film Critics, and a Golden Satellite Award for Best Picture, Comedy. It also made the top-ten lists of film critics across the country.

Still, *Malkovich* didn't quite cut it with the Academy of Motion Picture Arts and Sciences. Although the movie was nominated for three Oscars, the filmmakers went home empty-handed. While Cameron was obviously disappointed for the nominees, she had other things to do that night—like make her first appearance as one of Charlie's Angels. Along with her costars Drew Barrymore and Lucy Liu, Cameron presented the first award of the evening—Best Costume Design.

Cameron Diaz had truly arrived. Her paycheck for the upcoming *Charlie's Angels* was a whopping $12 million. Not bad for an actress who had only been in the business for five years—especially for someone who'd never sought a huge paycheck when looking for jobs.

By taking chances and mixing small, meaty roles with bigger, splashier ones, Cameron had done what every young performer in Hollywood dreams of doing—she'd made the A-list, that small group of stars able to command large paychecks and have their pick of projects.

She'd certainly come a long way from her cheerleading and party-hopping days in Long Beach, California. But you'll never find anyone more ready and willing to acknowledge her roots than Cameron Diaz.

2

CANDID CAMERON

Whenever Cameron talks about her upbringing, "fun," "laughter," and "noise" are words that always seem to factor into the mix. "I probably would have had a miserable childhood, walking around without that sense of humor in my family," she's observed.

Born on August 30, 1972, Cameron Diaz had the kind of childhood that makes it easy to understand her sense of humor and adventurous spirit. Her father, Emilio, and her mother, Billie, moved Cameron and her older sister, Chimene, from San Diego to Long Beach, California, when Cameron was very young. The town, known for having one of the largest naval bases in California, was always full of hustle and bustle—and men. It's no wonder Cameron grew up to be such a tomboy with all those military men all over town.

Her father, a second-generation Cuban immigrant, didn't treat his daughters any differently than if they had been boys, which definitely had a positive effect on Cameron. She has recalled that her research for 1999's *Any Given Sunday* was done when she was eight years old watching

---

Long Beach, California, is known for its busy port and large naval base. It's also Cameron's hometown. It was here that she developed her tomboy spirit, sense of humor, and laid-back approach to life.

football with her father. In fact, Cameron was a fan of both the Rams (who were based in Los Angeles at the time) and the San Diego Chargers.

"I grew up with football," Cameron once said. "My dad was a huge fan and he didn't have a son. So my sister and I absorbed that love of sports from him. My dad would wake up on a Sunday, yelling 'FOOTBAAAALL' even before his head came off the pillow." But it wasn't just a love of sports that her father instilled in Cameron. He also had an incredible sense of humor, which she undoubtedly inherited.

"My father's very sarcastic and dry," Cameron told *E! Online.* "When I was a kid, he was always playing around, saying things like, 'Get lost. Go play on the freeway.'" Obviously, he was kidding, but Cameron said that as a child, it was sometimes hard to tell whether he was serious. She and her sister had to learn the fine art of sarcasm pretty early on. But once Cameron figured it out, she ran with it, and has been a pro at comedy and deadpanning ever since. Through his humor, Cameron's father also taught her not to take herself or anyone else too seriously— a trait that influences Cameron's attitude about work, fans, and critics.

But it wasn't just her father who was joking around all the time—her mother was pretty laid-back and quick to laugh as well. Billie, of English, German, and Native American backgrounds, not only gave Cameron her blonde hair, blue eyes, and stunning cheekbones, but she also fostered a festive atmosphere around the Diaz household.

"My earliest memories are of laughter. I can shut my eyes and hear my father's laugh," Cameron has said. "My mother's is even more contagious. As a child I did everything I could to make her laugh because that would make me laugh too."

When they weren't busy having a good time, Cameron's parents were very supportive of their girls and gave them a lot of freedom. Cameron credits her parents for her independence and self-confidence. Both of Cameron's parents worked—her father as a foreman for an oil company, and her mother as an export agent—but they always made time for the family and still do to this day.

"I keep strong ties with my family and friends. The people in my life are very understanding," Cameron noted when talking about her crazy schedule. She even credits her parents with her recent decision to quit smoking. They mentioned to her that they'd realized she had smoked in seven of her movies, and it was enough for Cameron to sit up and take notice. "It was something to do with setting a bad example and it preyed on my mind," Cameron said in an interview. She learned parents can still teach you a thing or two when you're 28 years old and world famous.

But when Cameron was young, her parents seemed to face more of a challenge in trying to tame her wild side. Like many siblings, she and her sister had a serious love-hate relationship. They were constantly playing, fighting, running around, and acting like "goofs, dorks and freaks," Cameron admitted. But she didn't need her sister's help to be a cutup. She started to show her true colors at an early age. In second grade, while the rest of her classmates were throwing on plastic Princess Leia masks and witch hats for Halloween, Cameron dressed up as early Hollywood actress Mae West. Her outfit, complete with ridiculous amounts of plastic jewels, borrowed high heels, and a fake bust-line, turned a few heads. But that didn't bother Cameron.

At an early age, she had a significant growth spurt and, as happens to a lot of girls, was several inches taller than her male classmates by the time she reached middle school. Some kids in high school started calling her "Skeletor," after a superhero cartoon villain, because she was so tall and skinny. Although she was a beautiful blonde cheerleader at Long Beach Polytechnic High School, Cameron says that she was not a guy magnet during those years.

"I had no style . . . I was really obnoxious. I was just loud and probably unattractive," she's recalled. All the boys flirted with her in grade school, but in middle school and high school, she thinks they simply were not interested. "It's just starting to come back," Cameron said with a sly grin during an interview.

Even if the guys weren't looking her way in high school, Cameron has admitted that she was more than a little boy crazy. To add to the mix, she had some pretty odd tastes. "I always liked the boy who was sticking the needle through his hand or chopping up Sweet Tarts and snorting them," Cameron told *Vanity Fair* magazine. She even went over-the-top for love a few times. In the middle of the night, she drove by the house of one boy she had a crush on just to see if his car was out front.

Ever the party girl, Cameron got herself a beat-up Volkswagen bug when she was 16 and started party-hopping in Los Angeles with her friends. Her parents trusted her and gave her a little leeway—they even encouraged her obsession with heavy metal music. Her father was a Van Halen fan and her mom once accompanied Cameron to

Cameron's relationship with her older sister, Chimene (left), remains close. She credits family and friends with helping her stay grounded.

a Van Halen concert herself. Cameron says that today when she gets together with her parents, "It's like Surround Sound. It's really frightening."

But it wasn't always all fun and games. Cameron's parents made sure that their girls had a good education and learned about their heritage. She has yet to play a role that is specifically Latino, but Cameron has explained that she thinks there is already enough stereotyping in Hollywood and that's why she has avoided those parts.

Cameron has loved sports since she was a little girl. Here she is at the 1998 Toyota Grand Prix in Long Beach, California, where she and other celebrities raced identical Toyota Celicas to raise money for local hospitals.

"My Latin roots are very strong. All my life, because I'm blond and blue-eyed, people who aren't Hispanic can't believe that I am," Cameron recalled. "And people who are Hispanic always think I'm not, because I don't look like them. Being Latin is part of who I am and I bring that part to every role."

It seems that Cameron's parents taught her to have an open-minded attitude, which is probably why she has always refused to be pigeon-holed. Both in her career and in her personal life, the young actress has constantly stood up for herself and stuck to her guns—going after what she wants instead of doing what others may think is best.

Of course, Cameron's parents may have been a little upset with their own successful results when Cameron was 16 years old. That was when she came to them and told them she wanted to be a model. And in true Cameron style, she was not going to take no for an answer.

MODEL BEHAVIOR

If Cameron Diaz hadn't been the thrill-seeking, party-hopping teenager she was, Hollywood might never have heard of her. One day, Cameron and her friends were on a jaunt to L.A., driving from bash to bash, when she was approached by photographer Jeff Dunas. A less adventurous girl might have run for cover—or at least blushed and turned away—if a stranger had told her she should be a model. But not Cameron. As always, she was ready for an adventure, and modeling sounded like serious fun.

Dunas introduced his new "discovery" to all the right people, and within a week, Cameron had landed a modeling contract with Elite Modeling Agency, one of the most respected firms in the world. One minute she was spending her afternoons at cheerleading practice, and the next she was going to modeling auditions and strutting her stuff for ad agencies and catalogues. It didn't take long for Cameron to get work, but modeling wasn't the glamorous job most aspiring models dream of having. "I was a working model," Cameron explained, dismissing the idea that it was all fun and dress-up games. "I was doing junior ads for

Before Cameron gained fame as a highly talented actress, she was a hardworking, little-known model. She still has an interest in fashion today. Here, she arrives at a 1998 party given by famous fashion designer Calvin Klein in Paris.

newspapers every day of the week."

Paying her dues, Cameron finally landed some bigger jobs—ads for companies such as Levi's, Calvin Klein, Nivea, and Coca-Cola who wanted a young, fresh, American image. It was an image that agencies in foreign countries were also very interested in. Cameron's agent suggested she try modeling overseas. She might be able to make some real cash and get some exposure that could lead to more opportunities in the United States. Besides, world travel sounded like a way to have a pretty good time. Cameron was sold, but she had to convince her parents first.

It took a lot of smooth talking, but 16-year-old Cameron finally managed to get her parents' permission to go to Japan. She ensured them that the trip would be "super safe," but ended up hopping on a plane accompanied only by one other model, who was just 15.

Still, Cameron played the fearless girl and looked forward to walking off the plane and onto the covers of magazines. After all, Japanese casting agents loved tall blondes. But it wasn't quite as easy as she'd imagined it would be. When Cameron did get work in Japan, she could earn as much as $2,000 a day, but she didn't get work that often. And $2,000 doesn't last all that long when you're a teenager trying to support yourself and have a good time in an exciting, strange land.

"Believe me, you can get into a lot of trouble being 16 years old and in a foreign country with no adult telling you when to come home," Cameron told *Mr. Showbiz*. When she wasn't partying, however, Cameron took her career, or lack-thereof, very seriously. "It wasn't like, 'I'm so pretty.' It was more like, 'I can take advantage of this. I can travel and make money and get out of school.'"

The young model did take advantage of her situation. She left Japan and started country hopping. For the next five years she traveled all over the globe, working as she went, and having a good time everywhere. Her modeling career took her to Morocco, Mexico, Paris, and Australia, with pit stops back in the United States, where she finally landed a couple of *Seventeen* magazine covers and posed for *Mademoiselle*.

Still, Cameron is quick to point out that she was no supermodel, as some people like to say now that she's a star. She would rather not go around telling people she was something she wasn't. When she was in Paris, she worked twice in nine months. She says she worked very hard from age 16 just trying to make something

At 16, Cameron left home for Japan, hoping to land lucrative modeling assignments. Jobs were scarce and life wasn't quite as safe as she had told her parents it would be.

of herself. "Nobody can bring out any *Vogue* covers," Cameron told *Vanity Fair*. "If I had never told anyone that I was a model, no one would have known."

Eventually Cameron did make the United States her home base again, graduating from high school and settling down in California with her boyfriend, a video producer named Carlos de la Torre. The couple had met during Cameron's early modeling days.

When Cameron was 21 years old, she began to get a little bored with modeling—she felt a bit empty and unfulfilled. Luckily, that was just when her modeling agent suggested she try to make the transition into acting.

At first, Cameron thought it was a crazy idea. She knew that jumping from modeling to acting could prove to be painful and fruitless. After all, actors endure rejection on a daily basis, and many models had tried acting before only to fail miserably. But Cameron was never one to turn down a challenge, and she was more than ready for a change.

She went out on a few auditions—just testing the waters—and for months, she got nowhere. It was a little disheartening, so when Cameron was feeling ill on the day of the audition for a Jim Carrey film, *The Mask*, she almost didn't show up. She's said that she felt like a "stuffed pig," but she forced herself to go anyway. Amazingly enough, the audition resulted in Cameron's first callback.

Cameron was understandably excited. It was her first taste of success in the acting world. Little did she realize that the struggle was far from over. The young model with no acting experience was asked to come in and read over and over again. She didn't know what the filmmakers wanted from her, and she started to get frustrated with all the jumping through hoops.

At first, Cameron would do "anything the filmmakers wanted. . . . But it got to the point where I said, 'You know what? I'm not doing it anymore. I'm not going to practice with the choreographer so that he knows the steps he's going to teach the real girl who gets the job.'"

But the director of the film, Charles Russell, saw something special in the young woman and refused to let her quit. He demanded her best, and she finally delivered, turning in a solid performance. After that, Russell took up her cause with the producers of the film. Even though they originally wanted a more voluptuous actress, after 12 callbacks and investing in a padded, push-up bra, Cameron finally snagged the role.

Cameron has said that she felt like she was simply "in the right place at the right time." But she had no idea what she was getting into.

First of all, there was the larger-than-life, hyper star Jim Carrey—quite a personality to deal with on her first acting job. Carrey was constantly cracking Cameron up, making sure there was never a dull moment on the set.

"He is totally amazing and totally nuts," Cameron said, recalling those days working with Carrey. "He'd do his 'Somebody stop me' thing and I couldn't stop laughing. Then I'd compose myself and Jim would look at me out of the corner of his eye and then I'd collapse laughing again."

Not only did the young actress have to learn to control her funny bone, there was also the fact that she was playing Tina Carlyle, an over-the-top heartthrob with a seriously sexy wardrobe. The tomboy spent the entire shoot in high heels,

Her first role in The Mask *with Jim Carrey gave Cameron an ulcer, but the hit movie also brought her an agent, a manager, and a place on Hollywood's radar screen.*

tight dresses, tons of makeup, and padding to fill out her figure.

But none of these challenges compared to the uncomfortable realization that she was actually part of a big-budget film that a lot of people were banking on. "About a month into the movie, I said, 'This is kind of a big film, isn't it?' And they all said, 'Yes, Cameron. Yes it is,'" Cameron later recalled. When she realized the scope of the movie she was involved in, Cameron's body reacted to the stress with an ulcer, which was anything but fun.

Luckily, the extreme fear was all for nothing. *The Mask* was a hit, and Cameron landed on Hollywood's radar screen. She got an agent, a manager, and snagged ShoWest's (a prestigious convention for theater owners) Female Star of Tomorrow Award for 1996. In the past, the award had been won by Nicole Kidman and Julia Ormond, and it has since been won by Minnie Driver.

The struggling model had suddenly become a model-actress. So what did she decide to do with her newfound success? Grab a bunch of big-budget roles? Thrust herself into the spotlight? Take the money and run?

In a remarkably well-thought-out move, she told her manager and agent to play it cool. Even though she could have taken advantage of her situation, she didn't want to accept any lead roles. She explained, "I don't have any experience. I don't want to go straight into leading roles. I have too much to learn."

Suddenly, Cameron wasn't only about having fun. She was also about being smart—and building a solid foundation for an amazing career.

4

INDIE QUEEN

After *The Mask* hit it big, Cameron was offered a lot of roles—roles that were exactly like bombshell Tina Carlyle. As tempting as it was to jump at the parts simply to keep working, Cameron kept her wits about her. She didn't want to be typecast after her very first movie role. "I knew if I just took other parts that were exactly like Tina, I would end up not having much of a career," Cameron said. "I want to test what I'm capable of."

So when comedian Tom Arnold offered her a bimbo-ish part in *McHale's Navy*, a lowbrow comedy remake of a classic television show, Cameron turned it down. She did, however, decide to try out *Mortal Kombat*, the action picture that was a video game spin-off. Cameron had always been a physical person and loved to challenge herself athletically. When she was offered the part of Sonya Blade, she gladly accepted.

Then the young actress injured her wrist training for the role (she was karate-chopping her trainer's head) and had to back out. It was probably the best thing that ever happened to her career. Actress and former Miss Teen USA Bridgette Wilson took the role, and almost no one saw the movie.

Her lead role in the independent film Feeling Minnesota *was just one in a series of parts Cameron took that featured quirky characters and stretched her acting abilities. Working in independents also kept her from getting typecast.*

The wrist injury coupled with the unpleasant memory of that ulcer she'd suffered while filming *The Mask* soured Cameron on big-budget films. She decided to start auditioning for independent movies (films that are not backed by a major studio), where she would be able to relax a bit, learn more about acting, and have a little fun testing out odd characters and situations.

"I think that definitely your chances of coming across material in independent films—material that is more interesting and more challenging—is more likely than in big studio films," Cameron told Celebsite. "You always have to leave your doors open to independent films so that you have that opportunity." Her movie career barely begun, Cameron knew what she was doing and what she wanted.

Her first role after *The Mask* was in a very low-budget film called *The Last Supper*. The plot was the first of many twisted story lines Cameron would throw herself into over the next few years. Her character, Jude, and a bunch of other young, beautiful yuppies, have a dinner party at which they poison conservative right-wingers because they don't like the way they think.

At first, director Stacy Title and her fellow filmmakers wanted Cameron to play the part of the pretty, innocent Paulie, but Cameron wanted a challenge and asked to play the more vocal, slightly ruthless Jude. "I was surprised," Title said of her star's request. "She was so smart."

It was indeed a smart choice because Jude was a role Cameron could really sink her teeth into—one that would help her learn more about acting and playing different kinds of characters.

Next Cameron auditioned for another independent film (or indie), *Things to Do in Denver When You're Dead*, but lost the part to Gabrielle

Anwar of *Scent of a Woman*. That rejection didn't stop her. Cameron went out and snagged a role in writer-director Edward Burns's second film, *She's the One*. The movie, which costarred Burns and *Friends'* Jennifer Aniston, was hugely anticipated in Hollywood after the success of Burns's first homemade flick, *The Brothers McMullen*.

Cameron was psyched to be part of something so new and exciting and to be working with the director who was considered to be "the next big thing." But that didn't keep her from speaking her mind when she thought the storyline involving her character could use a little tweaking.

Cameron's character, Heather, is desired by a lot of men in the film. But the character seemed so cold and heartless, Cameron thought it was

In her third movie, She's the One, Cameron fought to change the script so that her character would be more likeable. From left: writer-director-actor Edward Burns with stars Maxine Bahns, Cameron Diaz, Jennifer Aniston, and Mike McGlone.

impossible to understand why all these men were after her. She believed that because the script made Heather such an unsympathetic character, all the men in the film looked ridiculous for being attracted to her.

"I gave Eddie suggestions about what I thought would serve the story better," she reported candidly. "He liked my ideas and went back and rewrote several scenes to make her more likable, without compromising the integrity of who she is."

Far from getting another ulcer, the young actress was starting to get more involved in the process of filmmaking. In just three films, she'd already come a long way. *She's the One* was a modest hit, and Cameron gained a lot of visibility, but she still didn't think of herself as a star. She would laugh at the idea of having fans, and was surprised when, during an interview for the film's release, an interviewer told her there was a website called the "Cameron Diaz Worship Page."

"No way—really?" Cameron said with a laugh. "I guess when you're working, you sort of keep focused on what you're doing. I haven't really experienced the fan thing yet."

Next Cameron won the lead female role in the independent comedy-drama *Feeling Minnesota,* which costarred Keanu Reeves. The first of many films in which Cameron's character got married, the film was shot in Minnesota, far from the glamorous surroundings of Hollywood. The young actress played a stripper-hooker who owes a loan shark money and pays back the debt by marrying one of his cohorts. Moments after the wedding, Cameron's character hooks up with her new husband's brother, played by Reeves, and runs off.

Her first day on the set, Cameron had to do a love scene with Reeves, but she says that wasn't the most daunting part of the day. She also had to jump right in to one of the most dramatic parts of the script—a monologue in which her character describes who she really is. "I was really scared I wasn't going to be able to do that as honestly as I wanted to," Cameron recalled. Compared to tapping into her character's soul on day one, love scenes were a piece of cake.

Feeling Minnesota might have been an odd experience—Cameron's character gets shot and left for dead on the side of the road—but Cameron said she also had her biggest laughs ever on the set. "I had this big makeout scene with Keanu Reeves that would have been OK except I'm in a wedding dress that he kept tripping over. It was just awful."

Personally, Cameron also met someone special while she was making the movie. Matt Dillon was in Minnesota at the time filming *Beautiful Girls*. They got to know each other, but Cameron says they didn't start dating until a year later. While in Minnesota, she was totally focused on her work.

Once *Feeling Minnesota* wrapped, Cameron moved on to another independent movie called *Head above Water*, in which she played veteran actor Harvey Keitel's wife. Released in 1996, the film has another strange plot involving betrayal and murder. She turned in a funny, vivid performance, but unfortunately, not too many people saw the film until it hit cable.

Next up was the small film *Keys to Tulsa*, in which Cameron had a tiny role. By the time the movie was released on video, the young actress had made a name for herself in Hollywood, so the filmmakers made Cameron look like she'd been the star of *Keys to Tulsa*. Her image was the prominent photo on the video's cover. She was annoyed that the marketing people were exploiting her fame. "That irritated me," Cameron said. "The producers took advantage . . . they used my name to sell the movie. That was unfair, especially to Deborah Unger, who was the female lead in it."

Not only was Cameron not taking lead roles, she was also refusing to make it look like she'd done lead roles. Of course, her next film would make it almost impossible for people to see her as anything but star material.

When Cameron took the supporting role of Kimmy Wallace in the Julia Roberts film *My Best Friend's Wedding*, she knew she was stepping out of independent films and into the spotlight of big-budget movies. But she also knew that this was Julia Roberts's film, and again, she was just ready to have a good time and learn. The first big shock for Cameron was how incredibly different it was to work on such a huge movie.

"There were a lot of difficult scenes in this film . . . acting with so many people around was a new experience for me," Cameron explained. "It was the first time I'd sat in a room of fifty extras and had to cry."

But crying wasn't the only hard part. The one scene that was more frightening than any other to her was the now infamous karaoke scene. Once the film wrapped, everyone wanted to know if she had been nervous, how many times she had to do the scene, and yes, if her singing really was that bad. Cameron said she's not as bad as Kimmy, but she's not great either. The filmmakers asked her to be awful, so her goal was to be as consistently bad as possible so she wouldn't have to sing it too many times. "That scene in the movie is as close as I will ever get to being a singer," Cameron admitted. "I felt bad

Cameron and Matt Dillon had been dating for about a year when the blockbuster hit My Best Friend's Wedding *was released. During interviews about the movie, Cameron patiently answered questions about their developing relationship.*

for the extras listening to me. They had to pay them more money that night," she joked.

Once again, Cameron had to get herself into a wedding dress for a movie, but this time, the problem wasn't other actors tripping over her skirt—it was the fact that she needed 10 people to help her carry around all the heavy tulle and taffeta. By the time the shoot was over, the young woman was tired of the whole wedding thing. Ever the tomboy, she couldn't wait to get out of the dress, and she admitted she was sick of saying the vows over and over again. She even said that she'd decided her own wedding was going to be a seriously simple affair.

In the famous karaoke scene from My Best Friend's Wedding, *Cameron intentionally sang terribly. "I felt bad for the extras listening to me," she joked. "They had to pay them more money that night."*

"I will probably just rent a bus and call my friends and see who's available," she declared. "'It's leaving in twenty minutes . . . Can you make it?'"

Even though the wedding and karaoke scenes were a challenge to film, Cameron did have several great experiences on the movie. Once again, she got to influence the direction of her character. She and many of her colleagues knew the final confrontation scene between Kimmy and Jules (Julia Roberts's character) didn't feel right. Originally, it had Kimmy crying and Jules lying again. Cameron wanted Kimmy to be more assertive. The screenwriters went back to the drawing board, and Cameron was relieved when they got a new scene in which Kimmy talks back to Jules, stands up for herself, and gets the truth out of her rival.

Once the shoot was finished, Cameron seemed to have a lot of good feelings about the whole experience. "I hope with all the work and love that went into making this movie, that people really enjoy watching it and get something from it," she said. "That's what you hope for. What it does for your career is ultimately not up to you."

What *My Best Friend's Wedding* did for Cameron's career was amazing. Not only did she eventually win a Blockbuster Entertainment Award for her role, but within days of the film's release, it seemed like everyone knew her name. People said she was the only person who could ever come that close to outshining Julia Roberts. Suddenly, Cameron was thrust into the spotlight, running around the country to premieres and doing interviews—which she claims she hates.

"It's like self-examination," she explained. "It just opens the door for all that ridicule." It didn't help matters any that at the time the movie was released, reporters had a whole other topic they were just dying to ask Cameron about—her romance with actor Matt Dillon. When *My Best Friend's Wedding* came out, Matt and Cameron had been dating for about a year, and the press couldn't ask enough questions about the couple that was constantly photographed holding hands and walking red carpets together.

Cameron took it all in stride, openly answering questions. "Matt's fantastic. He's had to deal with fame for a long time and he handles it sensationally," she said. "He's just like a regular guy. The friends he grew up with are still who he does everything with."

When interviews finally turned back to the topic of the film, Hollywood's new sensation was quick to talk about how much fun she'd had on the set of the movie, the friends she'd made, and what she'd learned from the world's biggest female movie star, Julia Roberts.

"One thing I realized from Julia . . . is that when you're the star of the film, the crew looks to you to set the tone of everyday work," Cameron said. "So when you come into work, whatever it is that you're giving off, that is what the tone is going to be for the working conditions."

Sounds like a lot of pressure and not a lot of fun, which may be one of the reasons Cameron still shied away from star vehicles after *My Best Friend's Wedding*, even though she could have headlined a big film. The young actress told the press that carrying a film just wasn't interesting to her. So with everyone still buzzing about *My Best Friend's Wedding*, she moved on to another independent ensemble piece, *A Life Less Ordinary*.

The movie, which reunited the writer, director, producer, and star of the British indie hit *Trainspotting*, was about a prima donna, played by Cameron, who gets kidnaped by a disgruntled former employee of her father's, played by Ewan McGregor. The plot intrigued Cameron, who was excited to begin filming.

"I can't wait," she told reporters. "I'm just out of my skin about it. I loved *Trainspotting*." The film didn't do quite as well as *My Best Friend's Wedding*. Reviewers and moviegoers didn't know what to make of its bizarre plot, but it did get nominated for an MTV Movie Award for Best Dance Sequence.

Still looking for funky, smaller projects, Cameron followed up *A Life Less Ordinary* with a very tiny role in another small movie, *Fear and Loathing in Las Vegas*. The relative failure of these two films didn't bother the actress.

Her return to big-budget movies with My Best Friend's Wedding *earned Cameron the 1998 Blockbuster Entertainment Award for Favorite Supporting Actress and gave her a chance to learn more about acting from superstar Julie Roberts.*

She had other goals in mind. "I personally couldn't care less about the box office success of a film," she declared. "I do movies for the experience. I don't care if anybody sees them."

But people were seeing her movies. In fact, her next big film took Hollywood by storm.

5

THE LITTLE MARY
THAT COULD

C ameron Diaz's rise to fame has often been compared to the careers of Julia Roberts and Sandra Bullock. All three superstars jumped around from small films to small roles in big films before breaking through with huge surprise hits. For Roberts it was *Pretty Woman*. For Bullock, it was *Speed*. For Cameron, it was *There's Something about Mary*.

No one had a clue that *There's Something about Mary* would be a hit in the summer of 1998. No one could have predicted that audiences would accept and even love a film that made fun of everyone from the mentally challenged, to the elderly, to average high school students. But they did. Cameron suddenly found herself at the center of a whirlwind media frenzy. And to think she almost didn't get the part.

According to *Entertainment Weekly*, Peter and Bobby Farrelly, the brothers who wrote the script and directed the film, did write the part with Cameron in mind. But during the audition process, they met another actress and completely fell for her. *Friends'* Courteney Cox was almost cast as the lead. Luckily, the Farrellys went with their original instincts.

Cameron almost lost the title role of There's Something about Mary *to* Friends' *Courteney Cox, but she won the part and turned in a performance that combined her wide-ranging comedic gifts with her dazzling beauty.*

"As we went on, we thought more of Cameron, especially after *My Best Friend's Wedding*," Peter Farrelly says. "She just had that glow."

The filmmakers offered Cameron the role, but her manager and agents weren't so sure she should take it. They saw the film's gross humor and irreverent script as sure career-killers for Cameron. "I'd find out from my manager that people had said, 'I can't believe you're letting her do that,'" Cameron told *Vanity Fair*. But as always, the young woman went with her gut. She thought the script was hysterical, and the lowbrow humor didn't bother her as much as it bothered the people who were there to advise her.

"I hang with guys, so it's easy for me to take on the gnarly stuff," Cameron explained. Since she was still seeking out roles that would simply allow her to have a good time, this was definitely the project to get involved in. "I didn't think, Where can I find a role that's going to get everybody in America to love me," Cameron said. "I thought, I want to go to work every day and laugh." That's exactly what she got.

She also ended up working for two directors who quickly fell in love with her—professionally, of course. Bobby seemed to be singing Cameron's praises on a constant basis. Her performance was so good, Bobby said, that "my brother, Pete, and I would be looking at each other like 'I don't know what to tell her.' We didn't know how to direct her and it was a little embarrassing. And sometimes we'd have her do it a different way just so we didn't look like total idiots."

The directors weren't the only ones on the set who were members of the Cameron Diaz fan club. The film gave Cameron and Matt Dillon, her then-boyfriend of more than two years, the

chance to work together. Cameron said she and Matt had always wanted to find a film in which they could both star, but they had thought it would be a romantic comedy where they would star as the lead couple. Once they both landed *Mary*, however, Cameron decided it was probably better the movie wasn't a big romance—that might have jinxed them. They were happy just to be able to spend so much time together.

Actually, Peter and Bobby Farrelly didn't hire Cameron and Matt because they were a couple. The brothers didn't even find out they were dating until they were all together on set. Once the Farrellys knew, however, they were excited to have two people on the set with so

Directors Peter (left) and Bobby Farrelly fell in love with Cameron's incredible acting abilities during the shooting of There's Something about Mary. *Here the three share a laugh at the movie's premiere.*

much chemistry. Matt would tease Cameron endlessly, trying to kiss her with his big fake teeth and generally acting like a goof ball.

"He'd kid around between scenes, like, 'Come here, baby. Give me a kiss.' I was like, 'Please just stay away from me,'" Cameron remembered. But she was so in love with Matt, she really didn't care about his appearance. She even told reporters she thought he looked sexy with his ridiculous caps. "There's no way this guy can look bad," she commented.

As much as Cameron loved the Farrellys and supported the film, she did have a few small problems with the script. The first was the infamous hair gel scene, but her objections didn't have anything to do with the gel itself. She thought the whole scene made her character look silly and dumb, when they'd spent the entire movie proving that Mary was a smart, together person.

"From Mary's point of view, she's not a stupid girl," Cameron said. "This is a big date, and to look that good you have to look in the mirror, right?" But she didn't protest, and once she saw the movie, she knew the Farrellys were right.

One thing she did put her foot down about, though. The original script called for Cameron to partially strip, and she wasn't about to do it. She told the Farrellys, "I don't think it's necessary. I'm a girl—I can make this sexy and not do the whole thing." She won that argument, and the movie didn't suffer because of it.

As much as Cameron insisted that she was behind *There's Something about Mary* all the way, she did have her moments when she had to pause and question what they were doing. "[The Farrellys] are out of their minds," Cameron said. "There were times when Ben, Matt, and myself were looking at each other like, 'Can we go this far? Is this really something we can live with as actors?'"

Apparently it was. And the stars probably didn't have a problem with being at the top of the box-office charts for eight weeks in a row in 1998. Cameron was on numerous magazine covers and was named *Entertainment Weekly*'s (*EW*'s) It Girl for the summer of '98. Once again, Cameron was thrust into the spotlight, with everyone in Hollywood and the press talking about her newfound superstardom.

Still, Cameron was reluctant to bask in all the attention. She downplayed her selection to *EW*'s It List by saying, "It's nice of them to include me on the list. I have a movie to sell, and they had a cover that was open . . . next year it will be someone else on the cover." When asked directly what it felt like to be a star, she answered, "The only time I know that is when someone in the industry says it to me."

The new sensation also didn't want people walking around saying that she was the lead in *There's Something about Mary.* "I just show up, do my little thing and leave," Cameron told *Premiere.* "Even with *Mary*, I didn't feel like I was carrying the movie. It was an ensemble."

That ensemble helped her win an MTV Movie Award, a Blockbuster Award, the New York Film Critics Award for Best Actress (for which she beat out eventual Oscar winner Gwyneth Paltrow), and a Golden Globe nomination.

At this point Cameron could no longer deny that she had fans. More Internet sites dedicated to her were popping up all the time. And Mary was such a guy's girl that boys and men started to obsess about Cameron, just as the characters in the movie had obsessed about Mary. Cameron never liked the idea of random strangers watching her every move, but she was as polite to her fans as possible.

"It's cute when you meet young boys and they're bright red and breathing like they've run up the stairs—but they're just sitting outside the door," she said. Because of *Mary*, many more people were approaching her, asking for her autograph, and snapping pictures. Cameron didn't mind as long as they asked.

Interviews were even more centered around her relationship with Matt Dillon, since the entire country had now had the chance to see them together in action. Both Cameron and Matt were gracious about answering questions. They never snapped or asked reporters to get back to the subject of the movie. Cameron told one reporter that she and Matt had a regular relationship, that they supported each other, and that she didn't think she could have made a lot of her recent decisions without his support.

"This is our life. We live it together," she said. "And it's important for me to feel he can rely on me—that he looks to me for support and vice versa." The couple was always affectionate in public and tried to live their lives as they would if they hadn't been famous.

Unfortunately, it wasn't long after the press junket for *Mary* that Matt and Cameron hit the rocks. Suddenly reports circulated that Matt had been seen out with other girls and that Cameron had been seen with other guys. Maybe *Mary* had jinxed them after all. Their relationship ended in 1999, and Cameron politely declines to talk about the details of the breakup to this day. Instead, she'd rather answer questions about her new boyfriend, Jared Leto, formerly of the television series *My So-Called Life*.

Actor Jared Leto, known for his role on the television series My So-Called Life, *is Cameron's current boyfriend. "We have a great time going out, dancing, doing things I really like," she's reported.*

"We have a great time going out, dancing, doing things I really like," Cameron said with a giddy smile. "With Jared I don't have to worry about his mood or whether he's feeling down all the time, like I did with a certain someone else."

Even though Cameron went through some changes in her personal life after *There's Something about Mary*, she didn't let the success of the film change her philosophy on work. She avoided potential blockbusters, choosing to continue with her philosophy that small films equal

After the success of There's Something about Mary, *Cameron returned to independent films with her appearance in the dark comedy* Very Bad Things, *a movie in which her character murders the best man on her wedding day.*

more fun. If anything, Cameron's choices became even more bizarre.

First up was the dark comedy *Very Bad Things.* This film was definitely an ensemble piece. Costarring Jon Favreau, Christian Slater, Jeremy Piven, and Daniel Stern, the movie is about a bunch of guys who mistakenly murder a call girl during a bachelor party. This event sets off a string of incidents that result in Cameron murdering the best man on her wedding day. If ever there was a role to prove Cameron was not ready to play a bunch of sweet girls like Mary, this was it.

Next the actress slipped in a quick stint on the set of the independent *Man Woman Film.* The movie was made by her friend Cameron

Pearson for a total of $38,000. Cameron made her cameo appearance as a favor and is seen for only a few minutes in the black-and-white picture.

Then, of course, came *Being John Malkovich*, which proved once and for all that Cameron was an actress who was willing to do pretty much anything in order to keep things interesting. When asked about the premise of the film, she said, "Life is an adventure. Certainly I think it would be interesting to just jump into somebody's head. If you jump into a random person, you have no idea what to expect. . . . You can never guess what's going to come next."

The young star might as well have been talking about herself. When it comes to her career choices, Hollywood can never guess what's going to come next.

And that's why they love her.

6

HOLLYWOOD'S ANGEL

During interviews for *There's Something about Mary*, Cameron was asked how the film had changed her life. Did she feel like the most popular actress in America? Was she snapping up movie roles left and right? As always, the California native was realistic about her answer.

"As far as work goes, it has changed, which is great," she said. "Who doesn't want to have a lot of options? But I know that it's not worth it to me to grovel and grab as much as I can. I'm just *not* in a race."

Cameron had spent years being smart about her career, and she wasn't about to stop now. Her gutsy choices caught the attention of Leonard Maltin, the *Entertainment Tonight* film reviewer and movie historian. "What has made her such a star at such a young age is her refusal to be stereotyped," Maltin said. "It shows what strength and showbiz savvy she has."

With her next few film roles. Cameron continued to illustrate her desire to avoid being pigeonholed. First up was Oliver Stone's *Any Given Sunday*. Not only did she

---

Cameron continues to make gutsy choices about the roles she accepts. Every part is different, whether it be the hard-driven football team owner, shown here with Al Pacino in Any Given Sunday, *the insecure Lotte Schwartz in* Being John Malkovich, *or the smart and sexy operative in* Charlie's Angels.

go directly from working with an unknown, inexperienced director in Spike Jonze, to a world-renowned Oscar-winner in Oliver Stone, but Cameron was also playing a character like none other she'd played before. As Christina Pagniacci, the owner of a professional football team and Al Pacino's boss, Cameron had to play a woman who was totally driven and would step on anyone to get what she wanted. "I didn't know where she was coming from," the actress said. "I don't have that sort of drive. I don't have that *want* to be No. 1."

But playing Christina wasn't the only challenge. Acting with Pacino was completely intimidating. The hard-working actress also had to film a scene where she walked through the locker room where a bunch of men were hanging out—naked. "On that day I kept both my eyes up and refused to be shocked by anything," she said with a laugh. The guys on the set were impressed by how unflustered she was. *Any Given Sunday* didn't have the best box-office take, but that didn't bother Cameron.

She went right from hanging with the guys to chilling with the girls in the low-budget ensemble film *Things You Can Tell Just by Looking at Her.* In this film, Cameron played a blind girl who was both a romantic and a cynic. The film gave the actress a chance to team up with some of her most respected peers, working with a cast that included Glenn Close, Holly Hunter, and Calista Flockhart. Then just when viewers thought Cameron was back in indie-film mode, she decided to make the big-studio film *Charlie's Angels.*

For a girl who insists she doesn't crave attention, doesn't care if people see her movies, and

Cameron struts on the ShoWest convention stage with Charlie's Angels
*costars Lucy Liu (left) and Drew Barrymore (right). The $12 million paycheck
Cameron received for the film gives her the freedom to continue to do
small-budget films as well.*

doesn't need to look sexy in front of the camera, this role may seem like an odd choice. *Charlie's Angels* has gotten more media attention than any movie in recent history. The stars—Cameron, along with Drew Barrymore and Lucy Liu—look like supermodels. But Cameron had a few pure, fundamental reasons for doing the film.

First, as always, it sounded like fun. Then Barrymore, who serves as one of the film's producers, decided she wanted to drop the Angels' guns and have them be martial arts experts instead. That definitely appealed to Cameron. "I love to kick butt. When I think back, I always have," she said. "The training and the exercise has brought out the tough girl who's never been far below the surface."

Perhaps the most important reason for taking the role is that Cameron was a huge Angels fan when she was little girl. At a recent Hollywood bash, Cameron found out that Farrah Fawcett, one of the original Angels, was attending also, so she begged a friend for an introduction.

Of course, the $12 million paycheck couldn't have hurt in the decision-making process. Having that amount of money in the bank will free Cameron up to do any small-budget film that catches her attention.

When talking about *Charlie's Angels*, the star is quick to point out that the film is different than the TV series. "The plot is based on the assumption that Charlie's Angels have always existed and we're just a new set of girls coming through," Cameron explained.

After *Charlie's Angels* wrapped, it was time for Cameron to go off to Italy to film the adaptation of Jennifer Egan's novel *The Invisible Circus*. In this film, Jordana Brewster of *The Faculty* plays Phoebe O'Connor, a teenager who goes to Europe to follow in the footsteps of her older sister, who died on her own trip overseas. Cameron plays Faith, the dead sister, and is seen only in flashbacks.

What's next for Cameron? First she's providing her voice for an animated film called *Shrek*. She's also been cast opposite Leonardo DiCaprio in Martin Scorcese's much-anticipated mob movie, *Gangs of New York*. She's even getting wired. Steven Spielberg is launching a website called POP.com for which Spielberg and director friends such as Ron Howard will produce short Internet films. Cameron was one of the first stars to sign on to be featured on the site, along with Steve Martin and Eddie Murphy.

As always, there's a lot going on with Cameron. But does she have anything other than acting on her mind? She's expressed that she would like to go to college, but not for the degree for which most people strive. She simply wants the knowledge that comes with education. She has also said that she's always been interested in zoology and photojournalism, so if she wasn't acting, she'd probably go on safari. Cameron believes that if she ever went to Africa, she might stay, and she doesn't want to give up on her career just yet. When it comes to daily life, Cameron would like to have Michelle Pfeiffer's career because "she works eight-hour days and only during the summer," but she hasn't mapped out a life plan.

"As far as being on a timetable in my career, I don't have any expectations really," Cameron confessed. Her goals are basic: to keep getting work and for that work to be interesting and challenging. But she always has things going on, such as her venture into the restaurant business. Cameron recently opened a restaurant called Bambu in South Beach, Miami, after falling in love with the area while she was working on *There's Something about Mary*. The food served at Bambu is inspired by the cuisines of Japan, China, Vietnam, and Thailand.

Whatever Cameron decides to do next, it's sure to be interesting, and it will probably be a smart decision. As her friend and costar Dermot Mulroney said, "Cameron is one smart cookie and she knows precisely what she's doing."

You can also be sure Cameron Diaz will be having fun while she's doing it.

CHRONOLOGY

1972	Born on August 30 in San Diego, California.
1988	Begins modeling.
1990	Starts dating Carlos de la Torre; graduates from Long Beach Polytechnic High School.
1993	Lands her first movie role in *The Mask*.
1994	*The Mask* is released.
1995	Stars in *The Last Supper*.
1996	*She's the One, Feeling Minnesota,* and *Head above Water* are released; wins the ShoWest Female Star of Tomorrow Award.
1997	*My Best Friend's Wedding* and *A Life Less Ordinary* are released.
1998	Wins the Blockbuster Entertainment Award for Favorite Supporting Actress for *My Best Friend's Wedding; There's Something about Mary* and *Very Bad Things* are released; wins New York Film Critics Circle Award for Best Actress for *There's Something about Mary;* nominated for a Golden Globe Award for Best Actress in a Comedy or Musical for *There's Something about Mary;* named one of *People* magazine's 50 Most Beautiful People.
1999	Wins Blockbuster Entertainment Award for Favorite Actress in a Comedy for *There's Something about Mary; Being John Malkovich* and *Any Given Sunday* are released; nominated for a Golden Globe Award for Best Supporting Actress in a Comedy or Musical for *Being John Malkovich*.
2000	Nominated for a SAG award for Best Supporting Actress for *Being John Malkovich;* wins American Latino Media Arts Outstanding Actress in a Feature Film Award and Blockbuster Award for Favorite Actress in a Drama for *Any Given Sunday; Things You Can Tell Just by Looking at Her* and *Charlie's Angels* are released.
2001	*The Invisible Circus* released; *Shrek* released; featured in "The Making of Shrek," a television special; participates in "America: A Tribute to Heroes" on television; *Vanilla Sky* released; honored at the 8th annual Women in Hollywood gala.

FILMOGRAPHY

1994   *The Mask*

1995   *The Last Supper*

1996   *She's the One*
        Feeling Minnesota
        Head above Water

1997   *Keys to Tulsa*
        My Best Friend's Wedding
        A Life Less Ordinary

1998   *Fear and Loathing in Las Vegas*
        There's Something about Mary
        Very Bad Things

1999   *Man Woman Film*
        Being John Malkovich
        Any Given Sunday

2000   *Things You Can Tell Just by Looking at Her*
        Charlie's Angels

2001   *The Invisible Circus*
        Shrek
        Vanilla Sky

2002   *Gangs of New York*
        The Sweetest Thing

AWARDS

1996   ShoWest Female Star of Tomorrow Award

1998   Blockbuster Entertainment Favorite Supporting Actress Award for *My Best Friend's Wedding*; New York Film Critics Circle Best Actress Award for *There's Something about Mary*

1999   Blockbuster Entertainment Favorite Actress in a Comedy Award for *There's Something about Mary*; American Comedy Award for funniest leading actress for *There's Something about Mary*

2000   American Latino Media Arts Outstanding Actress in a Feature Film Award for *Any Given Sunday*

FURTHER READING

Davis, Ivor. "Giddy, Gorgeous, and Just One of the Guys: Cameron Diaz." *Biography*, April 2000.

Heyman, J. D., and Marc S. Malkin. "Charlie's New Angels." *US Weekly*, March 27, 2000.

Hill, Anne E. *Cameron Diaz*. Philadelphia: Chelsea House Publishers, 2000.

Hofler, Robert. "The Year of Living Famously." *Premiere*, December 1998.

Neumaier, Joe. "Cameron Diaz." *Entertainment Weekly*, July 20, 1998.

Pearlman, Cindy. "5 Minutes With Cameron Diaz." *React*, July 14, 1997.

Peretz, Evgenia. "Frat-House Goddess." *Vanity Fair*, January 2000.

INDEX

PHOTO CREDITS:

Fred Prouser/Reuters: 2, 45; The Everett Collection: 6, 9, 52; Rose Prouser/Reuters: 11; New Millennium Images: 15, 25, 33; Chris Delmas/Zuma Press: 19; Danielle/Michelson/NewsCom: 20; Swan/Boomerang/NEWSMAKERS: 22; New Line Cinema/DPS: 28; Beitia Archives/Digital Press: 30; Vince Buck/AFP: 37; Columbia Pictures/DPS: 38; Howard Wager/OLUSA: 41; 20th Century Fox/DPS: 42; NEWSMAKERS: 49; PolyGram/DPS: 50; Steve Marcus/ Reuters: 55.

ABOUT THE AUTHOR

KIERAN SCOTT graduated with honors from Rutgers University in New Brunswick, New Jersey, with a B.A. in English and Journalism. She is the author of numerous young adult and middle-grade fiction and nonfiction books, including biographies on Leonardo DiCaprio, Matt Damon, and James Van Der Beek. Formerly the editor of popular young adult series such as SWEET VALLEY HIGH, ROSWELL HIGH, and FEARLESS, Kieran is now a freelance writer. Her favorite Cameron Diaz movies are *There's Something about Mary* and *Feeling Minnesota.*